Annie Smith Peck

Queen of the Climbers

by Marlyn Mangus

illustrated by Colin Bootman

Macmillan
McGraw-Hill
New York   Farmington

Book Design and Production: Kirchoff/Wohlberg, Inc.
Illustration: Dick Sanderson; Colin Bootman
Photography: 1, The Granger Collection; 2, Culver Pictures; 4-5, George Holton/Photo Researchers; 6 t.r., Brown Brothers; b.l., Culver Pictures; 7, UPI/Bettman

Macmillan/McGraw-Hill

A Division of The McGraw-Hill Companies

Macmillan/McGraw-Hill
1221 Avenue of the Americas
New York, New York 10020

Printed in the United States of America

ISBN 0-02-182169-0/5, L.11

8 9 DBH 02 01 00 99

Annie Smith Peck Queen of the Climbers

by Marlyn Mangus
illustrated by Colin Bootman

MACMILLAN / McGRAW-HILL

On September 2, 1908, a small, exhausted middle-aged woman climbed onto the snow-covered peak of Huascarán (wäs´kə rän´), the highest mountain in Peru. For Annie Smith Peck, then 57 years old, this moment fulfilled a dream of many years. She became the first person ever to climb one of the world's highest mountains. Standing atop Huascarán—22,205 feet (6,768 meters) tall—she was higher than any U.S. climber had ever reached in the Americas.

Born in Providence, Rhode Island, on October 19, 1850, Annie Smith Peck spent her life overcoming obstacles that would have defeated almost anyone else. In 1881, she earned a master's degree at a time when few women even went to college. When Annie then accepted a job teaching at Purdue University, she became one of the first women professors in the United States.

In 1884, Annie traveled to Europe to study. In Switzerland, she first glimpsed the Alps, a magnificent mountain range, and this encounter changed her life. She had always loved the sea, but from then on, she said, that love was "transferred for all time to the mountains." Soon she started climbing.

Her speed and grace in climbing were remarkable. A guide later declared, "She is a cat." For most of her climbs, Annie did little to prepare herself physically. When asked about training, she said that she "heartily recommended" it, but that she herself had "had no opportunity."

Annie returned to the United States in 1886 to take up a post as professor of Latin at Smith College. She continued climbing during vacations. By the time she left her teaching position at Smith in 1892, she had climbed many peaks in the United States, such as California's Mount Shasta.

In 1895, at the age of 45, Annie Peck returned to Switzerland to make a successful climb up the most famous mountain

in Europe, the Matterhorn (14,685 ft/4,476 m). Although two other women had already reached the summit, Annie Peck's accomplishment resulted in instant fame.

In part, that fame was due to her clothing. Annie did not wear the long skirts then considered the only proper dress for women. The climbing costume she wore instead—knickerbockers (pants ending just below the knees), puttees (strips of cloth wound around the legs), and a tunic (a long sweater extending below the hips)—caused a sensation throughout Europe and the United States.

Mt. Huascarán, Peru's highest mountain, is also an extinct volcano.

Having conquered the Matterhorn, Annie craved new challenges. She went to Mexico in 1897 and there climbed two of North America's highest peaks, Orizaba (18,700 ft/5,700 m) and Popocatépetl (17,887 ft/5,452 m). She made the climbs with surprising ease. To the disappointment of the newspaper for which she chronicled her climb, Annie made it up and down Popocatépetl ("El Popo") in a single day. She even stopped for a picnic lunch with a group of tourists on the way up!

4

After her success in Mexico, Annie set out to accomplish something different. Instead of following in the footsteps of other climbers, she now wanted to "attain some height where no man had previously stood." She wanted to be "first to the top" of one of the world's highest mountains.

The Andes mountain range in South America offered at least two exciting possibilities. At first Annie set her sights on Bolivia's Mount Sorata. She made two attempts to climb it, in 1903 and 1904, but both times disagreements broke out in her climbing party and she was forced to turn back. Annie then abandoned Sorata forever. Instead of choosing an easier mountain to climb, Annie Peck chose a tougher one. She decided to climb Peru's highest mountain, Huascarán, which is even taller than Mount Sorata.

Twin-peaked, Huascarán posed an incredible challenge. "The conquest of a mountain like Huascarán," Annie later wrote, "is a truly gigantic task. . . . The fact that 9,000 feet of snow must be surmounted, of which the lower edge is higher than the loftiest elevation in the United States

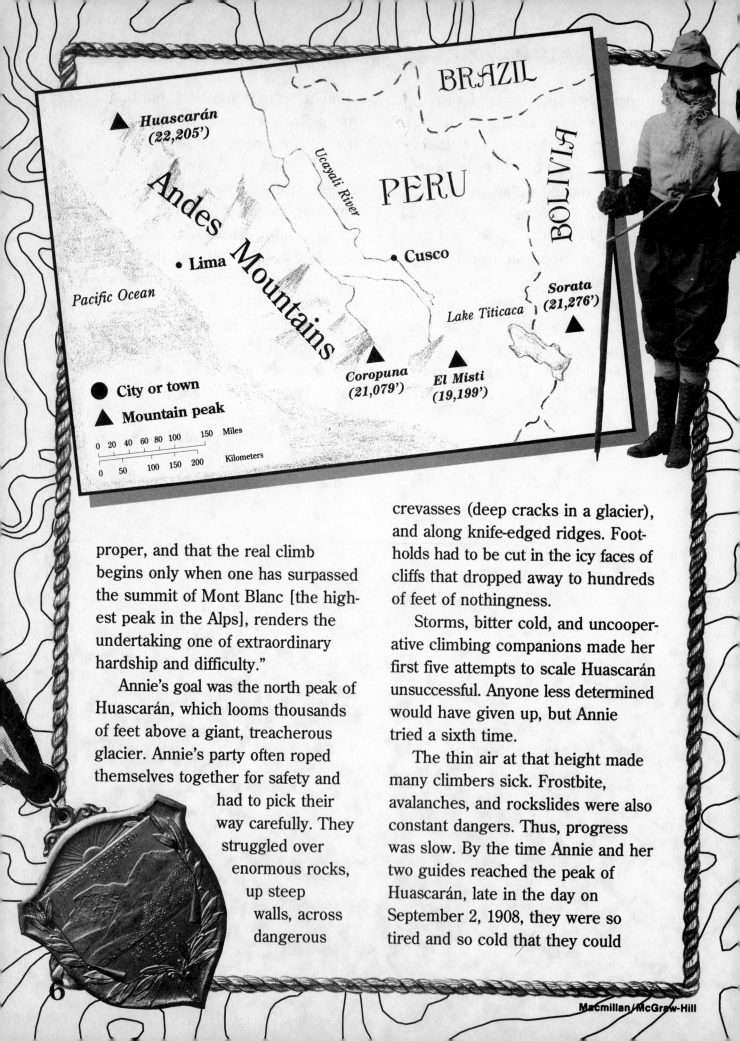

Map showing the Andes Mountains in Peru and Bolivia, bordering Brazil and the Pacific Ocean.

Huascarán (22,205')

Ucayali River

PERU

BOLIVIA

BRAZIL

• Lima

• Cusco

Pacific Ocean

Andes Mountains

Lake Titicaca

Sorata (21,276')

Coropuna (21,079')

El Misti (19,199')

● City or town

▲ Mountain peak

0 20 40 60 80 100   150 Miles

0   50   100   150   200   Kilometers

proper, and that the real climb begins only when one has surpassed the summit of Mont Blanc [the highest peak in the Alps], renders the undertaking one of extraordinary hardship and difficulty."

Annie's goal was the north peak of Huascarán, which looms thousands of feet above a giant, treacherous glacier. Annie's party often roped themselves together for safety and had to pick their way carefully. They struggled over enormous rocks, up steep walls, across dangerous

crevasses (deep cracks in a glacier), and along knife-edged ridges. Footholds had to be cut in the icy faces of cliffs that dropped away to hundreds of feet of nothingness.

Storms, bitter cold, and uncooperative climbing companions made her first five attempts to scale Huascarán unsuccessful. Anyone less determined would have given up, but Annie tried a sixth time.

The thin air at that height made many climbers sick. Frostbite, avalanches, and rockslides were also constant dangers. Thus, progress was slow. By the time Annie and her two guides reached the peak of Huascarán, late in the day on September 2, 1908, they were so tired and so cold that they could hardly enjoy their triumph.

Annie could enjoy her triumph later, though. Almost immediately, her feat was recognized by the nation of Peru. The president of the country presented her with a gold medal inscribed, "El Gobierno del Peru à Annie S. Peck—Nadie llegó antes que ella à la cumbre del Huascarán, 2 Stbre, 1908" ("From the government of Peru to Annie S. Peck—No one arrived before her at the summit of Huascarán, September 2, 1908"). And her feat was not forgotten. In 1928, the Lima, Peru Geographical Society named the north peak of Huascarán *Cumbre Ana Peck,* or "Annie Peck Peak." The peak is still known by that name today.

Annie continued climbing until she was eighty years old. It seemed that Annie would never wind down. In 1929, she set out on an exhausting seven-month airplane tour of South America. Determined to visit every country on the continent, she missed only one! The "heroine of Huascarán" was welcomed enthusiastically wherever she went.

Annie maintained a demanding travel schedule right up to the end of her life. In January 1935, Annie (now 84 years old) set out on a world tour. Unfortunately, poor health forced her to return to New York, where she died on July 18, 1935.

The great pilot Amelia Earhart was among those who paid tribute to this remarkable woman. "Miss Peck," she said, "would make almost anyone appear soft." Annie Smith Peck, queen of the climbers, had shown how much can be accomplished by someone whose daring and determination know no bounds.